TRYTHIS!
Photography

WITHDRAWN

Stephanie Turnbull

A+

Smart Apple Media

Published by Smart Apple Media, an imprint of Black Rabbit Books
P.O. Box 3263, Mankato, Minnesota, 56002
www.blackrabbitbooks.com

Printed in the United States of America, at Corporate Graphics
in North Mankato, Minnesota.

Designed and illustrated by Guy Callaby
Edited by Mary-Jane Wilkins

Cataloging-in-Publication Data is available from the Library of Congress

ISBN 978-1-62588-374-2

Photo acknowledgements
t = top, b = bottom, l = left, r = right, c = center
page 1 InesBazdar; 3 Catalin Petolea; 4 wavebreakmedia; 5l taelove7,
tr wavebreakmedia, c eungchopan; 6l MANDY GODBEHEAR,
r jwblinn, 6b Lucky Irene/all Shutterstock; 7t Mim Waller, b Kiselev Andrey
Valerevich/Shutterstock; 8 Mim Waller; 9l and r David Ionut,
b stocker1970/all Shutterstock; 10t Mim Waller, l chillchill_lanla,
r kropic1; 11t Jane Rix, b leungchopan; 12t Dan Kosmayer, c baranq,
b Sura Nualpradid; 13t iofoto, bl Art Konovalov/all Shutterstock;
13br Mim Waller; 14t aodaodaodaod, c HixnHix, b Matteo Cozzi;
15t tomgigabite, b Pan Xunbin; 16t Norikazu, b l to r Alex Kosev,
Matt Ragen, mountainpix, POORMAN, William J.Mahnken/all
Shutterstock; 17t and r Mim Waller, l Orla, c Pinkcandy, r and br racorn;
18tc pukach, tr Kostenko Maxim/all Shutterstock, b Mim Waller; 19 Mim
Waller, 20t Guy Callaby, l Darrin Henry, r Pavel L Photo and Video; 21t
aslysun, tl YanLev, tr braedostok, bl Ingvar Bjork, b Lukiyanova Natalia /
frenta, br second corner; 23 Aleksandr Kurganov/all Shutterstock
Cover top right Twin Design, background PHOTOCREO Michal Bednarek,
main image Estelle/all Shutterstock

DAD0062b
012016
9 8 7 6 5 4 3 2

Contents

Why try photography?

Photography is a fantastic hobby. Here are a few reasons to try it!

1 It's easy to do.

It's not hard to take super snaps—all you need are a few basic skills. Keep your camera handy to get plenty of practice.

Hold your camera still with both hands, so you don't take crooked or blurred photos.

2 You don't need expensive gear.

Experts use big, fancy cameras, but all you need is an ordinary **compact camera** or decent-quality **camera phone**.

Compact cameras are light to carry and easy to use.

3 You can get creative.

Ever thought of taking extreme close-ups, arty angles, or amazing **abstract** shots? Be brave and try new things.

Taking photos from unusual angles can make objects look more dramatic.

4 It's lots of fun.

Photos of your friends and family make great gifts and displays—and silly selfies keep you all smiling!

Now test out the brilliant projects in this book and see for yourself how exciting photography can be. Look out for the helpful tips and extra ideas.

People pictures

Take fantastic photos of your friends using these top tips. Take plenty, then keep the best.

1 *Decide on the best place to take your photos. A clear space works better than a busy, confusing background.*

2 *Think about light. Is it so sunny that people are squinting, or so shadowy you can't see their faces? Move people so light comes from the side.*

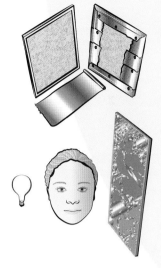

*Get rid of shadows by making a **reflector**. Pin foil around a cork board. Stand it to one side of your friend (with a light on the other side) to bounce light back onto their face.*

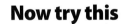

3 *Ask people to move their heads together. This makes a better shape and looks more natural.*

Now try this

Find silly things for people to wear, then take photos of everyone looking relaxed and happy.

Always check first that people want you to take their photo.

Stunning scenery

One of the best times to take photos is on vacation. Here's how to make your pictures look professional.

Buy a case for your camera to protect it when you travel.

1 *First, think about what to photograph and whether it's better as a tall (portrait) image or a wide (landscape) shot. If in doubt, try both. You might be surprised how different things can look.*

This tall shot highlights the boat, while the wide shot shows all the windmills.

2 *Now imagine lines splitting your camera screen into thirds, across and down. This technique is called the* **rule of thirds***.*

Position objects on or near these lines instead of in the middle. This can make them look more interesting.

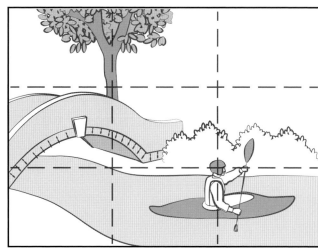

A higher horizon makes the sea more impressive in this scenic shot.

Now try this

Try to place important parts of the photo on the four points where the imaginary lines cross. They will stand out even more.

Clever close-ups

Don't stand back and try to cram too much into your photos—get up close instead and capture amazing details.

1 First, check whether your camera has a **close-up setting**. This photographs near objects in much sharper **focus**.

2 Look for the most impressive details of the object or scene. Make them stand out by using the rule of thirds (see page 9) or let them fill the frame completely.

Statues look far better close up!

A zoom button just enlarges a section of the photo, which won't be very good quality. Move closer instead.

Lots of identical objects look great close up and in sharp focus.

3 *Remember that ordinary objects can look fascinating when viewed close up. Try peering into a box of cookies, a jar of candy, or a pile of leaves.*

Now try this
Take extreme close-ups of everyday objects and ask friends to guess what they are.

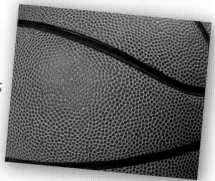

Amazing angles

If you want to take really impressive photos, don't just stand there—change position!

1 *Try looking down at things from above. This could mean standing on a chair or steps. You'll get a whole new view and see shapes and patterns you might have missed before.*

Everyday things can be striking when viewed from above.

2 Now crouch as low as you can, or lie down and look up. This angle makes people, buildings, and other objects seem bigger. It's also a great way of showing detail on small things such as flowers.

The wispy tops of this wheat crop stand out against a blue sky.

Now try this

Look down at your feet and photograph them on different backgrounds!

3 Try tilting your camera at an angle to make ordinary scenes look a little strange.

Choose an angle that suits your subject.

Arty ideas

Instead of trying to show whole scenes or objects, focus on lines, curves, colors, and textures to create beautiful abstract images.

1 *Go outdoors and hunt for shapes and patterns. You might see swirls in sand, snow, or tree bark, fantastic cloud formations or cracks in paving stones.*

2 *Take a close-up (see pages 10-11) of a striking piece of the pattern. Don't try to include too much.*

The size of this shell doesn't matter—just its wonderful curves and spirals.

3 *Add a little blurriness and mystery to your image by taking it in dim light or through a rainy window.*

Now try this
Try using a black-and-white setting, if your camera or phone has one, to create really bold pictures.

Show feelings through photos. Gray swirls may be sad, while colorful splashes burst with energy.

Your camera may have a low-light or night setting for dull days. Don't always use the flash.

Funny faces

Great photos don't have to be serious. Find some funny faces and take snaps that make you smile.

1 *See if you can spot windows, doors, and other features on buildings or machinery that look like faces. Photograph them carefully, avoiding bits that aren't part of the face.*

2 *Find pairs of googly plastic eyes and stick them onto everyday objects to create your own characters. You might be surprised how much personality they have!*

Search for objects with head shapes to stick eyes on!

3 *You could also slice and arrange fruit or vegetable pieces on paper plates and photograph them from above.*

Now try this

Ask your friends to stand against a blackboard or whiteboard, then draw details behind them. Get them to make their funniest faces for some really silly shots!

Be careful with knives when chopping up food!

Camera-free photos

You don't always need a camera to take photos. Here's a clever method using a computer scanner.

1 Choose a fairly flat, clean object. Flowers, leaves, keys, coins, and jewelry scan well.

2 Position the object on the scanner.

3 Close the lid. For a more colorful background, lay a sheet of colored paper or card over the object first.

Be very careful not to scratch the screen.

4 Scan the image. If the cover won't shut properly, don't look directly at the bright light—it could damage your eyes.

5 Save the image on the computer. Print it or use it as a desktop background.

Now try this

Buy some **light-sensitive paper** and place objects on top. Leave in sunlight for about 15 minutes, then hold the paper under running water. It turns dark blue, except for the areas that have been covered. This a great way of making stylish prints.

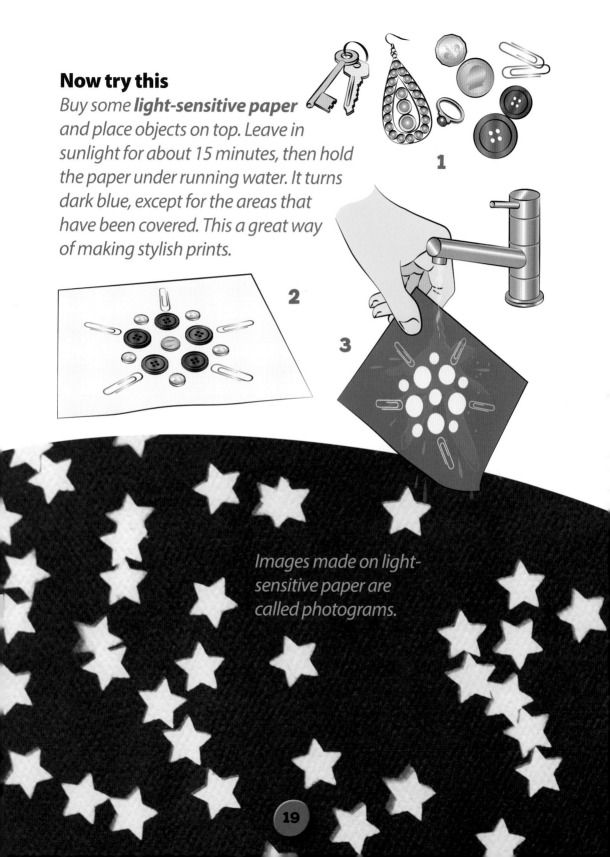

1

2

3

Images made on light-sensitive paper are called photograms.

Photos on show

Don't leave photos on your phone or camera and forget them—print and display your favorites.

1 *First, upload photos to a computer and use a program such as Adobe Photoshop to make them look as good as possible. This could include lightening shadows or removing* **red eye***.*

Photos look more professional without the glare of red eye.

2 Crop *photos to position main features better or get rid of parts you don't want.*

Trim any empty space at the sides of images by resizing photos on screen or cutting them with scissors.

Don't always show whole figures—try focusing on the top half.

3 Have photos printed, put them in frames, and hang or stand them in your bedroom. Framed photos also make great gifts. Use **mounts** to make images stand out.

Upload photos regularly in case you accidentally delete them from your camera.

Now try this

Try cutting up photos and creating a **photo montage** on your bedroom wall. You could also make scrapbooks with pictures and extra decorations.

Glossary

abstract
Not showing the whole shape of objects, scenes, or people, but picking out striking colors, shapes, and patterns.

camera phone
A camera built into a cell phone. Many are simple, but those in smartphones can be great quality. You can download apps that let you create effects such as colored filters, borders, or even outlines that turn images into cartoons.

close-up setting
A camera setting you select to make near objects stand out in sharper focus. Half press the shutter button to let the camera focus. It will beep when it's ready. Then press the button down fully to take the photo.

compact camera
Small cameras that usually take better quality photos than cell phones. Some have useful settings, for example for taking close-up images, night shots, or moving objects.

crop
To trim a photo so that only the most important section is left.

flash
A quick flash of light from your camera that makes a dull or dark scene brighter. Sometimes this may make your photo too bright, so experiment with turning it off.

focus
In clear, crisp detail; not blurred.

light-sensitive paper
A type of thick paper that changes color in sunlight.

mount
A piece of backing card to display a photo against.

reflector

reflector
A white, silver, or colored surface. Many photographers use lightweight, circular reflectors that fold up neatly.

photo montage
A display made up of lots of photos.

red eye
The effect of having glowing eyes in photos. It happens when a camera flash reflects off the back of eyes in dim light.

rule of thirds
A way of composing pictures by placing objects off-center to make them catch the eye better. Look at photos in magazines or paintings in galleries and you'll see how often this is done.

www.digitalphotography4kids.com
Find lots of information in this digital photography guide.

www.ephotozine.com/article/10-top-tips-for-taking-better-photos-with-camera-phones-18339
Read hints and tips for taking photos with your cell phone.

www.clickitupanotch.com/2012/07/photography-for-kids
Learn more about photography skills and try out some great activities.

Index